WILD BACKYARD ANIMALS

Watch Out! ALLIGATORS!

Harper Avett

PowerKiDS press.

New York

Published in 2016 by The Rosen Publishing Group, Inc.
29 East 21st Street, New York, NY 10010

First Edition

Editor: Caitlin McAneney
Book Design: Katelyn Heinle

Photo Credits: Cover Matt Hansen Photography. Dynamic Wildlife Photography/Moment/Getty Images; back cover, pp. 3, 4, 6, 8–10, 12, 14, 16, 18, 20, 22–24 (background) Polovinkin/Shutterstock.com; p. 5 Juan Gracia/Shutterstock.com; p. 6 Erni/Shutterstock.com; p. 7 (main) Rudy Umans/Shutterstock.com; p. 7 (map) Volina/Shutterstock.com; p. 9 (alligator) ullstein bild/Getty Images; p. 9 (crocodile) defpicture/Shutterstock.com; p. 11 Marianne W. Dent/Shutterstock.com; p. 13 Millard H Sharp/Science Source/Getty Images; p. 14 Matt Tilghman/Shutterstock.com; p. 15 CCimage/Shutterstock.com; p. 17 mark higgins/Shutterstock.com; p. 19 romarti/Shutterstock.com; p. 20 John Wollwerth/Shutterstock.com; p. 21 Melissa King/Shutterstock.com; p. 22 Greg and Jan Ritchie/Shutterstock.com.

Library of Congress Cataloging-in-Publication Data

Avett, Harper, author.
 Watch out for alligators! / Harper Avett.
    pages cm. — (Wild backyard animals)
 Includes index.
 ISBN 978-1-5081-4275-1 (pbk.)
 ISBN 978-1-5081-4256-0 (6 pack)
 ISBN 978-1-5081-4257-7 (library binding)
 1. Alligators—Juvenile literature. I. Title.
 QL666.C925A94 2016
 597.98'4—dc23
                                    2015023513

Manufactured in the United States of America

CPSIA Compliance Information: Batch #BW16PK: For Further Information contact Rosen Publishing, New York, New York at 1-800-237-9932

CONTENTS

ALLIGATOR COUNTRY

Alligators are big-toothed predators that are best left alone. These animals wandered Earth alongside dinosaurs about 80 million years ago! Their strong tail and **armored** body make them amazing wild animals. But what happens when you find them in your backyard?

Problems between people and alligators happen when people construct houses and other buildings in alligator **habitats**. People who live in alligator country need to be on the lookout around lakes, swamps, and rivers. After all, that's the alligator's backyard.

AMERICAN ALLIGATORS USED TO BE ENDANGERED, BUT THEIR NUMBERS ARE GROWING.

ALLIGATOR HABITATS

Will you find an alligator in your backyard? That depends on where you live. There are two species, or kinds, of alligators in the world—the Chinese alligator and the American alligator. Chinese alligators live only in the Yangtze River valley in China.

American alligators are found in freshwater in warm areas of the southeastern United States, such as Louisiana and Florida. They like to sunbathe along the banks of freshwater bodies, such as rivers. Then, they dive into the water for a meal. In this book, we'll focus on the American alligator.

CAIMAN

BACKYARD BITES

Caimans are part of the alligator family. They're found in Central and South America.

AMERICAN ALLIGATOR TERRITORY

UNITED STATES

ATLANTIC OCEAN

A MAJOR ALLIGATOR HABITAT IS THE EVERGLADES, WHICH IS A TROPICAL WETLAND AREA IN SOUTHERN FLORIDA.

BUILT FOR SURVIVAL

The American alligator's body is built for survival. It has thick scales, called scutes, covering its body. The scutes act like a coat of armor. Though it has short legs, the alligator is a great swimmer. It can also run short distances on land. Growing up to 15 feet (4.6 m) long, the alligator is one of the biggest predators in its habitat.

An alligator's tail is very strong. It helps the alligator swim through water. It also stores fat for the winter. This **muscular** tail is also used as a **weapon**.

ALLIGATORS USE THEIR POWERFUL JAWS TO CATCH PREY AND HOLD ON TIGHT. THEIR JAWS ARE STRONG ENOUGH TO CRACK A TURTLE'S SHELL.

CROCODILE

ALLIGATOR

BACKYARD BITES

You can tell an alligator and crocodile apart by the shape of their snout, or nose and jaw. Alligators' snouts are shaped like the letter "U," while crocodiles' snouts are shaped like the letter "V."

BEASTS ON THE HUNT

Alligators aren't just built for survival. They're built for the hunt, too. Alligators are usually nocturnal hunters, which means they mostly hunt at night. They usually hunt in the water. They have a special body part in their throat called a glottis. It helps them capture prey without swallowing too much water.

On land, an alligator might wait quietly near the water's edge. When an animal comes to the edge, the alligator will run at it and pull it under the water. That's a hunting trick called ambushing.

ALLIGATORS OFTEN HOLD THEIR PREY UNDERWATER UNTIL IT STOPS FIGHTING.

BACKYARD BITES

Alligators usually swallow small animals in one piece. However, they often hold large prey tight in their mouth and spin wildly in the water to tear off pieces.

UNLUCKY PREY

Alligators are at the top of the **food chain** in their habitat. That means they have few natural predators and many natural prey. Alligators are carnivores, which means they mostly eat meat. Any animal living in an alligator's territory is possible prey.

Alligators like to hunt fish and turtles in the water. They also hunt snakes and mammals, big or small. This is bad news for animals that come to the water's edge to take a drink. They may end up ambushed by an alligator!

YOUNG ALLIGATORS ARE PREY FOR BIGGER ANIMALS SUCH AS BOBCATS, RACCOONS, AND BIRDS. EVEN OTHER ALLIGATORS MIGHT EAT THEM!

BACKYARD BITES

If you live in alligator territory, don't let your dogs or cats run loose. Alligators are known to eat people's pets.

AN ALLIGATOR'S LIFE

These huge hunters start out inside small eggs. A mother alligator can lay more than 50 eggs at a time. She covers the eggs with plants until they **hatch**. Young alligators live in groups. While adults also spend time in groups, they're not as friendly. Alligators **communicate** through roars, coughs, and deep calls.

Female alligators usually spend about two years taking care of their young. They stay in their home range. However, males often wander farther, maybe even into backyards.

BACKYARD BITES

When an alligator hatches, it's already up to 8 inches (20 cm) long.

A GROUP OF ALLIGATORS IS CALLED A CONGREGATION.

WATCH OUT!

Sometimes humans and alligators cross paths. Alligators like water and may wander into backyards that have ponds or other bodies of freshwater. Some people even keep alligators in their backyards as pets, which usually requires a **license** to be legal.

Alligators may become **aggressive** when approached by humans. They might snap at or bite people who get too close. There have been around 20 proven deaths by alligator since 1948. In July 2015, a man was killed by an alligator in Texas after ignoring signs that warned of nearby alligators.

THE FLORIDA FISH AND WILDLIFE CONSERVATION COMMISSION SAYS THAT THERE ARE AROUND SEVEN ALLIGATOR ATTACKS EVERY YEAR.

BACKYARD BITES

Alligator attacks do happen, but they're not usually deadly. Between 1973 and 1990, there were only five deaths from alligator attacks in Florida.

ALLIGATOR SAFETY

Many times, alligator attacks can be avoided. People visiting parks and wetlands with alligators sometimes get too close or even throw things at the alligators. Sometimes people feed wild alligators, which makes the alligators less afraid of people.

How can you stay safe? Make sure your backyard is fenced so alligators can't get in. Stay away from waters known to have alligators. If you're in these waters, be aware of what's around you. If you see an alligator, stay far away.

IF AN ALLIGATOR EVER ATTACKS, FIGHT BACK. SINCE AN ALLIGATOR IS COVERED IN ARMOR, TRY TO HIT OR POKE ITS EYES, NOSE, OR EARS.

If an alligator is close by, run away from the water. The alligator will only chase you if it can pull you into the water.

WARNING

ALLIGATORS

KEEPING ALLIGATORS SAFE

At one time, the American alligator was at serious risk of dying out. Luckily, animal specialists have worked hard to keep this awesome animal alive. Today, the American alligator isn't endangered, but it's still at risk of dying out someday.

People are the biggest risk to alligators. They destroy alligator habitats by building in them or polluting the water. Some people hunt alligators, even though it's illegal in some states. Alligators are sometimes hunted for their skin, which is used to make shoes and purses.

BACKYARD BITES

Alligators can live almost 50 years in the wild.

TO KEEP ALLIGATORS SAFE, PEOPLE NEED TO KEEP ALLIGATOR HABITATS CLEAN AND SAFE FROM DESTRUCTION.

A BIG PART TO PLAY

Alligators play a big part in their **ecosystems**. They keep populations of other animals under control. By eating their natural prey, alligators provide balance in their habitats.

Alligators may be scary creatures, but they should be treated with respect. It's good to stay away from alligators. If you see one in your backyard, call the authorities to have it removed safely. If you see one in nature, let it go about its business. It's got hunting to do, and it's best to stay away from these beastly biters!

GLOSSARY

aggressive: Showing a readiness to attack.

armored: Covered with hard skin or pieces of metal.

communicate: To share ideas and feelings through sounds and motions.

ecosystem: All the living things in an area.

endangered: In danger of dying out.

food chain: A line of living things, each of which uses the one before it for food.

habitat: The natural home for plants, animals, and other living things.

hatch: To break open or come out of.

license: An official paper that gives someone permission to do something.

muscular: Having large muscles, which are parts of the body that allow movement.

prey: An animal hunted by other animals for food.

tropical: Warm and wet.

weapon: Something used to fight an enemy.

INDEX

WEBSITES

Due to the changing nature of Internet links, PowerKids Press has developed an online list of websites related to the subject of this book. This site is updated regularly. Please use this link to access the list: www.powerkidslinks.com/wba/alli